T0137604

Venice Is Vegan

For the Animals

PAIGE GALVAN

AuthorHouse™
1663 Liberty Drive
Bloomington, IN 47403
www.authorhouse.com
Phone: 833-262-8899

Because of the dynamic nature of the Internet, any web addresses or links contained in this book may have changed since publication and may no longer be valid. The views expressed in this work are solely those of the author and do not necessarily reflect the views of the publisher, and the publisher hereby disclaims any responsibility for them.

Any people depicted in stock imagery provided by Getty Images are models, and such images are being used for illustrative purposes only. Certain stock imagery © Getty Images.

This book is printed on acid-free paper.

ISBN: 978-1-6655-0854-4 (sc)
ISBN: 978-1-6655-0853-7 (e)

Library of Congress Control Number: 2020923359

Print information available on the last page.

Published by AuthorHouse 11/19/2020

authorHOUSE®

Venice Is Vegan

For the Animals

PAIGE GALVAN

This is Venice. Venice does not eat meat or any animal product. She is Vegan. Venice says the animals are her friends not food.

Venice knows that she can get plenty of protein and healthy nutrients from fruits, vegetables, nuts, grains and meat alternatives like tofu or tempeh.

When people eat meat that means a sweet innocent animal was killed just so that human could have a snack. This makes Venice sad so she chooses other snacks. There are lots of yummy vegan snacks!

Venice does not drink cow's milk or eat dairy cheese. She knows there are other options like almond milk or oat milk and plenty of vegan cheeses to choose from.

Cow's milk comes from a mommy cow whose baby was taken away from her so that humans could steal her milk that was supposed to feed her new baby. This is very very sad for the mommy and baby cow. Venice would not want to be taken from her mommy so she knows it's not fair to do that to the animals.

Eating a vegan diet keeps Venice Every healthy and happy and it keeps the animals healthy and happy too! That is why Venice is vegan for the animals.

Printed in the United States
By Bookmasters